THE CHANGING CLIMATE OF ASIA

Patricia K. Kummer

NORTH AMERICA

SOUTH AMERICA

EUROPE

ASIA

AFRICA

AUSTRALIA

ANTARCTICA

Cavendish Square

New York

CN950
Kummer

Published in 2014 by Cavendish Square Publishing, LLC
303 Park Avenue South, Suite 1247, New York, NY 10010

Library of Congress Cataloging-in-Publication Data
Kummer, Patricia K.
The changing climate of Asia / Patricia K. Kummer.
p. cm. — (Climates and continents)
Summary: "Provides comprehensive information on the geography, wildlife, peoples, and climate of the continent of Asia and the changes taking place there as a result of climate change"—Provided by publisher.
Includes bibliographical references and index.
ISBN 978-1-62712-443-0 (hardcover) ISBN 978-1-62712-444-7 (papeback) ISBN 978-1-62712-445-4 (ebook)
1. Asia—Environmental conditions—Juvenile literature. 2. Asia—Geography—Juvenile literature. 3. Asia—Social conditions—Juvenile literature. 4. Climatic changes—Asia—Juvenile literature. 5. Climatic changes—Social aspects—Asia—Juvenile literature. I. Title.
GE160.A78K86 2014
363.7095—dc23
2012015926

Editorial Director: Dean Miller
Senior Editor: Peter Mavrikis
Copy Editor: Cynthia Roby
Art Director: Jeffrey Talbot
Designer: Amy Greenan
Photo Researcher: Alison Morretta
Production Manager: Jennifer Ryder-Talbot
Production Editor: Andrew Coddington

Expert Reader: Victor Savage, associate professor, Department of Geography, National University of Singapore

The photographs in this book are used by permission and through the courtesy of: Cover photo by Jade/Blend Images/Getty Images, Universal Images Group/SuperStock; Universal Images Group/SuperStock, 4; Mapping Specialists, 6; Adrignola/Pangea continents and oceans/Pangaea continents.svg/ Creative Commons Attribution-Share Alike 3.0 Unported license, 8; Thien Do/Photo Library/Getty Images, 9; Stock Connection / SuperStock, 12; Mapping Specialists, 13; Michele Falzone / Jon Arnold Images / SuperStock, 14; PORNCHAI KITTIWONGSAKUL/Staff/Getty Images, 15; AP Photo/Anupam Nath, 16; Eye Ubiquitous / SuperStock, 18; AP Photo / Xinhua, Du Huaju, 19; T. BALABAADKAN -UNEP / Still Pictures / The Image Works, 22; Blum Bruno / Prisma / SuperStock, 24; © Arterra Picture Library / Alamy, 28; © Arco Images GmbH / Alamy, 28; ZSSD / SuperStock, 30; De Agostini / SuperStock, 31; © Travel Pix Collection, 34; Peter Adams/The Image Bank/Getty Images, 36; imagebroker.net / SuperStock, 39; © Francois Werli / Alamy, 42.

Printed in the United States of America

CONTENTS

THE LARGEST CONTINENT

Looking at a globe, or at a world map, it is quite easy to find the seven **continents**. They are Earth's largest land areas. Asia is the largest of the seven continents. In order of size, the other six continents are Africa, North America, South America, Antarctica, Europe, and Australia.

Getting To Know Asia

Asia covers about 30 percent of Earth's land area. This huge continent stretches from the Arctic Ocean in the north to the Indian Ocean in the south. Asia's eastern lands touch the Pacific Ocean. To the west, Asia is separated from Europe by the Ural and Caucasus mountains and by the Caspian, Black, and Mediterranean seas. To the southwest, the Suez Canal and the Red Sea separate Asia from Africa.

This photo taken from a satellite in space captures Asia's immense size—the largest of the seven continents.

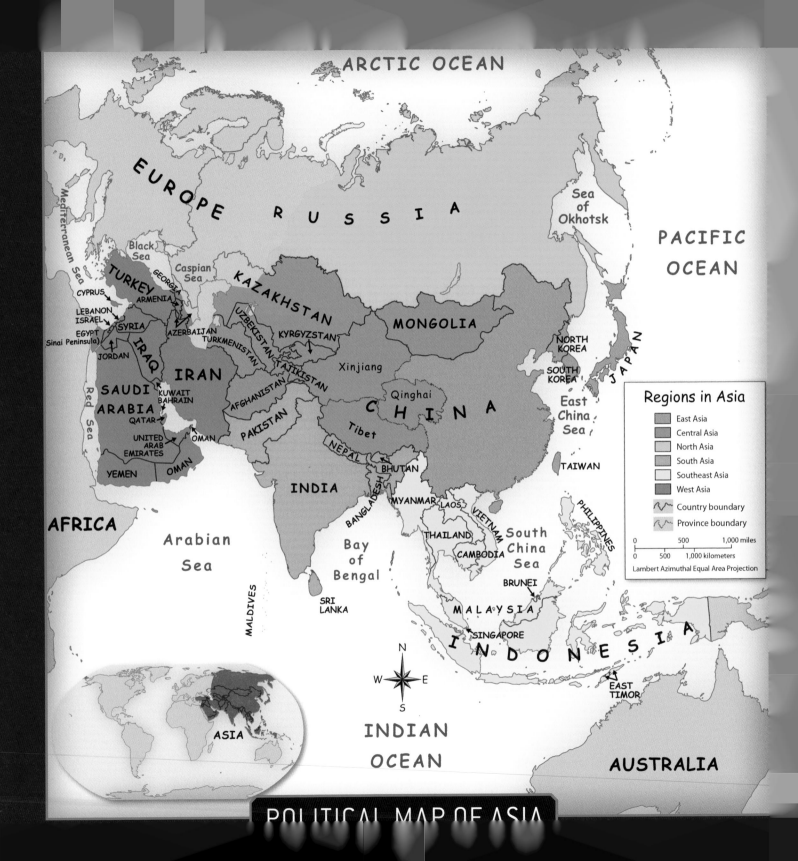

POLITICAL MAP OF ASIA

Where in the World Is Asia?

Use the political map on page 6 to answer the following questions about the continent of Asia:

1. Which five countries are in both Asia and Europe?

2. Which country has land in both Asia and Africa?

3. Which country has the greatest amount of land in Asia?

4. Which country has land in two regions? What are those regions?

5. Which region is closest to Australia?

6. Which region is bordered by the Bay of Bengal and the Arabian Sea?

ANSWERS:
1. Russia, Kazakhstan, Turkey, Georgia, Azerbaijan
2. Egypt
3. Russia
4. China / East and Central Asia
5. Southeast Asia
6. South Asia and Southeast Asia

Asia's large landmass is often divided into six regions—North, East, Southeast, South, Central, and West Asia. North Asia is also called Siberia. The regions share some features in common, such as land, climate, or people.

Because of Asia's huge size and location, the continent has many climate zones. Each has its own weather conditions—from **cyclones** to **typhoons** and from wet to dry **monsoons**. In turn, Asia's many climates provide **habitats** for a wide variety of plants and animals.

Asia also has the world's greatest number of people. Its population is made up of thousands of ethnic groups. People from an ethnic group share a language and culture and live in a specific area. A few of Asia's ethnic groups are the Arabs of West Asia, the Mongols of Central Asia, and the Hmong of Southeast Asia.

The Continents and Change

For hundreds of millions of years, Asia and the other continents have undergone slow and steady change. In fact, about 250 million years ago, there was only one continent— Pangaea. Gradually, Pangaea broke apart, and the seven continents that we know were formed. Asia was the last continent to gain its final shape. That occurred about 25 million years ago.

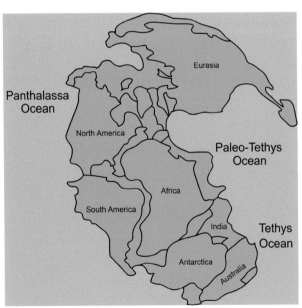

About 250 million years ago, the supercontinent of Pangaea contained all of Earth's land. Continental drift split this huge landmass into the seven continents.

Phong Nha-Kè Bàng National Park

Phong Nha-Kè Bàng National Park is located in north-central Vietnam. In 2003 it became a UNESCO (United Nations Educational, Scientific and Cultural Organization) World Heritage Site. Some of Asia's oldest limestone formations, including hundreds of caves carved by underground rivers, are located in the park. Scientists have traced the limestone back 464 million years. Those formations help explain Earth's history. The different layers of limestone show when major movements of Earth's tectonic plates occurred. The layers have also recorded the shifting routes of the caves' underground rivers. Fossils in the caves' walls have left a record of the ancient plants and animals that lived there.

Earth and its continents continue to change. Earth's crust is made up of many **tectonic plates**. These hard, rigid sheets of solid rock are always moving. Sometimes they crash into each other. These plate collisions can create mountains. Other plate movements cause earthquakes to occur or volcanoes to erupt. Asia has experienced many of these disasters.

Another kind of change that concerns Asia and the other continents is **climate change**. Climate change is caused in part by how people use the land. Asia's large population has needed to make intensive use of its land. To gain more farmland, people have cut down forests. They have also turned grasslands into cropland. Those changes have harmed the natural environment and have led to climate change. With fewer forests and grasslands, much of Asia now has warmer temperatures and less rain. Today, Asia's leaders and individual people are working to improve the environment. Their actions are still bringing more changes to Asia.

TWO

RISING MOUNTAINS, SINKING COASTLINES

By 160 million years ago, most of Asia had taken its current shape. Only South Asia and the Arabian Peninsula were missing. At that time, South Asia was a huge island. The Arabian Peninsula was attached to the continent of Africa.

About 50 million years ago, the Indian Plate moved north and slammed into the Eurasian Plate. The world's highest mountains—the Himalayas— began to form as a result of the collision of these plates. About 25 million years ago, the Arabian Plate pulled away from Africa. Then, it crashed into what is now Turkey and Iran in West Asia. Finally, the continent of Asia as we know it today was completely formed.

Some of Asia's land is still moving. India pushes north about 2.4 inches (6.1 cm) each year. The Arabian Peninsula moves north and east about 1.6 inches (4.1 cm) each year. All of these tectonic shifts are pushing Asia farther east.

Mountains and Plateaus

About 75 percent of Asia is made up of mountains and plateaus. The Pamir Mountains are known as the Heart of Asia. They meet and form a "knot" with other mountain ranges that are some of the world's highest. These mountain ranges extend from China in East Asia into Turkey in West Asia. They form a barrier between the land north and south of them. The Ural Mountains run north to south, forming part of Asia's boundary with Europe.

Asia's mountain ranges have either grown or shrunk through the years. The Himalayas, the world's youngest mountains, have gotten taller. They increase in height about 0.4 inches (1 cm) each year as South Asia's tectonic plate continues to push north. Mount Everest, the world's highest point at 29,035 feet (8,850 m) above sea level, is part of the Himalayas. The Urals, on the other hand, are an old mountain range. **Erosion** from wind and water continue to wear them down.

As you can see from the physical map of Asia on page 13, mountain

Snow-covered Mount Everest rises in the Himalayas between Nepal and the Tibet region of China.

ARCTIC OCEAN

East
Siberian
Sea

Bering
Sea

PACIFIC
OCEAN

Laptev
Sea

Kara Sea

Kolyma
River

EUROPE

Siberia

URAL MOUNTAINS

Ural R.

Ob River

Yenisey River

Lena
River

Sea
of
Okhotsk

Mediterranean Sea

Black
Sea

Caspian
Sea

CAUCASUS MTS.

Aral
Sea

Amur
River

Lake
Baikal

Hokkaido

Honshu

ALTAY MTS.

Gobi Desert

Sea
of
Japan

Korean
Peninsula

Euphrates R.

Tigris R.

ZAGROS MTS.

Persian Gulf

PAMIR
MTS.

TIAN SHAN

Taklimakan
Desert

KUNLUN SHAN

Yellow
River

East
China
Sea

Red Sea

Arabian
Peninsula

Indus River

HIMALAYA

Plateau
of Tibet

Yangtze River

Taiwan

Mount Everest
(29,035 ft., 8,850m)

Ganges River

AFRICA

Arabian
Sea

Deccan
Plateau

Ganges
Delta

Bay
of
Bengal

Mekong River

Philippine
Islands

South
China
Sea

Elevations in Asia

Feet	Meters
Over 10,000	Over 3,050
5,001–10,000	1,526–3,050
2,001–5,000	611–1,525
1,001–2,000	306–610
0–1,000	0–305
Below sea level	Below sea level

▲ Mountain peak

Country boundary

Province boundary

0   500   1,000 miles
0   500   1,000 kilometers

Lambert Azimuthal Equal Area Projection

Borneo

Celebes

Ceram

New
Guinea

Sumatra

Java

Timor

Sumba

ASIA

N
W   E
S

INDIAN
OCEAN

AUSTRALIA

PHYSICAL MAP OF ASIA

ranges encircle most of Asia's major plateaus. The Tibetan Plateau, known as the Roof of the World, is the world's largest and highest plateau. It continues to rise even higher. As South Asia pushes northward against the Himalayas, the plate collision lifts up the Tibetan Plateau.

Tall mountains surround the Tibetan Plateau, which is the source of many of Asia's major rivers.

Plains, Steppes, and Deserts

Plains, steppes (grasslands), and deserts cover the other 25 percent of Asia. The map on page 13 shows that those lands are often next to one another. Because they are neighbors, changes in one area can affect the land and environment in the others.

Asia's plains have the continent's richest soil, largest forests, widest river valleys, and many valuable mineral deposits. Those natural resources make it possible for great numbers of people to live and work on the plains. The plains' level lands are ideal places to build Asia's large cities. The plains' rich soil allows farmers to plant large areas with wheat, corn, rice, and sugarcane. In some areas, farmers have worn out the soil by planting the same crops year after year. With the need for better cropland, farmers cut down trees in nearby forests. **Deforestation** also occurred when mining companies cut down trees to dig deep, **open-pit mines**. These mines are giant craters that allow Asia's coal, iron ore, tin, bauxite,

In central Thailand, farmers harvest a crop of jasmine rice from a paddy.

copper, and gold to be brought to the surface faster, easier, and at a lower cost than through underground mining.

Asia's steppes are treeless areas covered with thick grasses. They border the continent's deserts, which are huge areas of sandy or rocky land. The world's largest petroleum (oil) deposits are under the Arabian Peninsula's sands. Oases in the deserts have grasses, date trees, and watering holes. On the steppes and in the deserts, herders move their livestock from place to place so the animals can feed on the grasses. When animals graze for too long in one area, the grasses are destroyed.

Asia's deserts are getting bigger. Grasses on nearby steppes are disappearing. Neighboring plains are becoming less able to produce crops. Forests are being destroyed, and trees are not being replanted. As those changes take place, **desertification** occurs. Desert sands spread over the bare plains and steppes.

Rivers, Lakes, and Coastlines

Most of Asia's major rivers begin on its plateaus. Then, they cut through valleys and plains before emptying into Asia's gulfs, seas, and oceans. **Deltas** have formed where some rivers empty into coastal waters. The Ganges Delta

Indian villagers carry their belongings through floodwater in an effort to reach higher ground.

Where the Rivers Flow

MAPPING SKILLS

Study the physical map of Asia on page 13 to answer the following questions:

1. Why do you think Siberia's major rivers flow north into the Arctic Ocean?

2. Name the rivers that flow from the Tibetan Plateau.

3. Why do you think there are no major rivers on the Arabian Peninsula?

ANSWERS:
1. Major mountains prevent them from flowing south or east.
2. Yellow, Yangtze, Mekong, Irrawaddy, Indus, Brahmaputra and Ganges
3. It's desert land.

is the world's largest delta. When Asia's rivers flood, rich soil for farming is left behind on the plains and deltas. But floods can damage crops and homes. To prevent harmful floods, hundreds of dams have been built on Asia's rivers.

Most of Asia's lakes are **reservoirs**. Although Asia has few natural lakes, those it has are large—Lake Baikal, Lake Balkhash, the Aral Sea, the Caspian Sea, and the Dead Sea. The seas are really salt lakes. The Aral

Rusting ships now sit abandoned on dry land that was once part of the Aral Sea.

Three Gorges Dam

Asia's longest and the world's third-largest river is the Yangtze. During the past two thousand years, it has caused severe floods. To prevent this flooding, China built the Three Gorges Dam. The dam's name comes from the three nearby scenic **gorges** through which the Yangtze winds. Completed in 2008, the dam had already prevented several major floods.

Everything about the Three Gorges Dam is huge. Its construction cost $30 billion and required the muscles of about 250,000 workers. The dam's wall is 610 feet (185 m) tall and stretches 1.3 miles (2 km) from one side of the Yangtze to the other. The reservoir that sits behind the dam covers 244 square miles (632 sq km) of land. The Three Gorges Dam also is the world's most powerful hydroelectric power plant. It can generate more electricity than any other dam.

Sea, once the world's fourth-largest lake, is shrinking. It lost most of its water after dams were built on the rivers that flow into it. Now, salt flats lie in place of the water. When winds blow over the flats, they carry salt to nearby land, harming farms. Less water has made summers hotter and winters colder near the lake.

Asia's long coastline continues to be shaped by wind and water. Heavy wave action caused by monsoon winds has worn away parts of the coast. **Tsunami** waves have permanently moved beaches and put some islands underwater. Rising sea levels are causing the Yangtze, Ganges, and Mekong deltas to sink. Land on the Yangtze Delta has sunk about 10 feet (3 m). All of those coastal changes have led to flooding, causing towns to sink and people to lose their homes.

THREE

WARMING TEMPERATURES, VARYING RAINFALL

Asia has a variety of climate zones. They range from the dry, bitterly cold Arctic to the hot, steamy tropics. Hot, dry desert climates are also found throughout the continent. Asia's most extreme recorded temperatures are 129.2°F (54°C) in Tirat Tsvi, Israel, and -90°F (-68°C) in Oimekon, Russia.

Much of Asia's weather is caused by monsoons. The winter monsoons come from the north. They bring cold, dry weather to East Asia. They can also create dust storms in Central and West Asia. The summer monsoons blow up from the Indian Ocean. They bring heat, humidity, and rain to South, Southeast, and southern East Asia. Asia's mountains prevent the hot, wet air from traveling north.

During the past one hundred years, Asia's temperatures have increased because of climate change. Its temperatures have gone up even more than those in the rest of the world. Asia's precipitation (rainfall and snowfall) has changed, too. In some areas, such as Thailand and Bangladesh, heavier monsoon rains have caused more severe flooding of farmland and city streets. Other areas, such as northwestern China, have gone through long **droughts**. In those places, the ground becomes hard. Crops will not grow.

In India, a farmer waters by hand plants that are growing in cracked, drought-stricken earth.

What Has Caused Climate Change?

Major, long-lasting differences in temperature and precipitation patterns are known as climate change. In part, people cause climate change. As Asia's population has grown, people have moved into places where humans had not lived before. To build farms, towns, and large cities, they have cut down large areas of Asia's forests. They have also pushed into dry grasslands in Central and West Asia. Changes made to forests and grasslands affect the climate. Temperatures increase and rainfall decreases.

In addition, Asia's homes, apartments, factories, and office buildings must be heated and cooled. Great amounts of wood, charcoal, coal, oil, and natural gas are burned for heat and for

How Scientists Measure Climate Change

Scientists measure climate change in many ways. Throughout Asia, they use thermometers and rain gauges at weather stations to record temperature and precipitation. They compare this data to data from the past. In Mongolia, they study growth rings from two-thousand-year-old trees. The rings tell when there have been rainy and dry periods in the past. On the Tibetan Plateau, they drill into glaciers and study ice cores. These studies show that the past fifty years have been the warmest ones in the last one thousand years.

Mongolia's Gobi Desert

In August 2010, Mongolia's prime minister and other leaders went on a field trip. They traveled to the southern part of Mongolia's Gobi Desert. Under the hot sun, they held a meeting about climate change. Five years earlier, the government leaders would have seen herders grazing their goats on that land. Now, the land is empty. Sands have spread over the grass. Through desertification, the grassland has become part of the Gobi Desert.

Overgrazing the land has led to climate change. Since 1940 the temperature in the area has increased by 3.78°F (2.1°C). That is a huge increase in a short time. The world's average temperature has only increased about 1.3°F (0.74°C) in the past one hundred years. Rainfall in this area has decreased. Seven severe droughts have occurred since 2000. The Gobi's few rivers and lakes have dried up. These conditions have led to the death of thousands of livestock. The herders and their families must find other ways to make a living.

cooking. In the past fifty years, the number of gasoline-powered cars, motorbikes, and trucks in Asia has increased. All of those fuels give off carbon dioxide, which leads to climate change and causes air pollution.

Results of Climate Change

Throughout Asia, the warming climate has affected the environment. Both the amount and depth of ice in the Arctic Ocean have decreased. In parts of Siberia, temperatures have increased about 2.4°F (1.3°C). This warming has caused the **permafrost** to melt by several inches (cm) each year. Siberia's land has become soft and wet, causing hundreds of buildings in Siberia's cities to sink. In addition, Siberia's Lake Baikal has ice cover about sixteen fewer days each winter.

Since the 1970s, the temperature in the Himalayas has increased by about 2°F (1.1°C). Glaciers in the Himalayas are retreating (melting) about 50 feet (15.2 m) a year. Water from the melting glaciers has caused rivers and lakes to flood.

Natural Disasters

Asia experiences many natural disasters because of its location. Volcanoes, earthquakes, and tsunamis occur because of activity deep within Earth's crust. The force of those activities hits the eastern and southern parts of the continent especially hard. Those lands are near the Ring of Fire, an area in the Pacific Ocean where volcanic eruptions and earthquakes occur. Lava from volcanic eruptions destroys nearby property. But lava also enriches the soil. Years later, crops, trees, and other plants again cover the ground.

Earthquakes cause great damage to homes and other structures. Most of that damage can be repaired. Other changes are permanent. In March 2011, a 9.0-strength earthquake caused the eastern coastline of Japan's Honshu Islands to drop about 4 feet (1.2 m). Honshu also moved 8 to 12 feet (2.4–3.7 m) closer to North America. Because the earthquake occurred under the ocean floor, it caused a tsunami. The wave reached as high as 133 feet (40.5 m) and brought seawater inland as far as 6 miles (9.7 km). The rush of water destroyed towns, ruined farmland, and killed at least 15,800 people.

Asia's other natural disasters are caused by typhoons and cyclones. These severe windstorms start over warm water near the Equator. Typhoons form over the western Pacific Ocean. Cyclones develop over the Indian Ocean. In those areas, warm, wet air rises and starts spinning. The Philippines, Vietnam, China, and Japan experience many typhoons. Cyclones strike along both of South Asia's coasts. When typhoons and cyclones make landfall, their winds cause much damage. The winds can reach 200 miles (322 km) per hour. Heavy rains from the storms cause severe floods. Those storms can wash away coastlines, damage sand dunes, and ruin forests.

FOUR

A CHANGING NATURAL ENVIRONMENT

Nature and people have made many changes to Asia's land and bodies of water. In turn, those changes have affected the habitats of the continent's plants and animals.

Falling Forests

Siberia is home to the world's largest forest. It is big enough to cover the United States. At one time, larch trees spread throughout the far north. Now, warmer temperatures are causing them to die. Fir, spruce, and pine trees are spreading northward, replacing the larch. Those new trees provide more heat to the ground. That causes the permafrost to thaw, which in turn leads to even warmer temperatures. In other parts of Siberia, forests have disappeared completely. They have been destroyed by logging, mining, and drilling for oil and natural gas.

As parts of Siberia's forests are disappearing, animals such as the Siberian tiger are losing their natural habitat and becoming endangered.

Many birds and large animals make their homes among Siberia's trees. As the variety of trees has changed and the number of trees has decreased, some animals have lost their homes. They are now **endangered species**. The Siberian tiger, the Far Eastern leopard, and the greater spotted eagle are a few of them.

Southeast Asia is home to the world's oldest tropical rainforest.

Dipterocarp trees form a large part of the rainforest. Orchids and ferns grow on those trees. Strangler figs wind around the trees' trunks. Silvery gibbons live in the dipterocarps' high branches. They feed on the figs. Large areas of dipterocarp, kapok, tualang, and teak forests have been cut down by logging companies. As those trees disappear, so do the plants and animals that depend on them. Today, the rainforest's orangutans, Malayan tapirs, tigers, rhinoceros, and Asian elephants are endangered species.

The Asian elephant is an endangered species as its home in Asia's tropical rainforests disappears.

Siberia's Protected Forest

Forests cover about 95 percent of the Central Sikhote-Alin UNESCO World Heritage Site in southeastern Siberia. This area is now protected from logging and other activities that could harm the land. Siberian larch, Korean pine, and many kinds of fir, spruce, ash, oak, birch, and elm trees grow there. Other plants sprout below the trees. The forest provides a rich habitat for many of Asia's endangered species. Siberian tigers, Asiatic black bears, brown bears, Eurasian lynxes, and reindeer feed on plants and small animals found in the forest.

Fewer Grasslands, Drier Deserts

A variety of grasses and small shrubs grow on Asia's steppes. Bactrian camels (the two-humped kind), gazelles, saiga (a kind of antelope), and wild horses graze on the grasses. Burrowing animals such as voles and jerboas dig homes in the soil. Imperial eagles, lesser kestrels, and black vultures feed on the small animals.

Desertification of Asia's steppes is causing grasslands to disappear. In turn, this reduces the habitat of the Przewalski's horse.

Today, the grasses in some steppe areas are disappearing. Asia's farmers plowed the grasses under and planted crops. During long droughts, the crops died, leaving bare soil. In other steppe lands, herders allowed livestock to overgraze. These farming and herding practices have turned some steppe lands into dust. With less grass to eat, the Bactrian camel, the saiga antelope, and the Przewalski's horse are now endangered species.

Climate change has caused the deserts of Central and West Asia to receive less rain and snow than before. This has decreased the variety of large wild animals living in West Asia's deserts. Oryx and gazelles are now endangered. The honey badger, jackal, and striped hyena have become extinct in the region. When rains do come, the deserts' plants store water. For example, the Gobi Desert's saxaul tree traps water behind its bark. Birds and other animals tap into the bark for a drink of water.

Polluted Lakes, Rivers, and Coastlines

Asia's lakes, rivers, and coastlines provide homes for many fish,

Lake Baikal: No Pollution — Yet

Currently, Lake Baikal, the world's deepest lake, has Asia's clearest, cleanest water. The lake is the only home of the world's only freshwater seal—the Baikal seal. Oilfish swim in the lake before being eaten by Baikal seals. Bullheads, omul (a type of salmon), perch, eelpouts, and sturgeons also live in the lake. Efforts are being made to keep this lake free from pollution.

birds, and other wildlife. Many of these waters have become polluted. Oil leaking from nearby wells and pipelines has polluted the world's largest lake, the Caspian Sea. The sturgeon that once filled the lake are now endangered.

Dams have harmed the habitats of other animals. After dams were built on the Yangtze River, the Yangtze River dolphin became extinct. The Yangtze's finless porpoise is now endangered. The lake known as the Aral Sea was once full of carp, perch, and pike. Flamingoes, pelicans, and a variety of ducks nested on its shores. When the rivers that fed the lake were dammed, those animals died or flew away. Recently, another dam was built to bring water into part of the lake. Some of the fish and birds have now returned.

West Asia's coastlines have suffered from leaking oil and other pollution. Along Asia's southern coasts, many mangrove trees grow. Their roots prevent coastal erosion by slowing down the flow of river water into the oceans. Fish, shrimp, crabs, and snails breed among the trees' submerged roots. Monkeys, lizards, sea turtles, and shorebirds feed on the fish and shellfish. But pollutants from the rivers have killed many of the mangroves. This has led to erosion and to the loss of habitat for many animals.

FIVE

PEOPLE AND CHANGE

f all the continents, Asia has the largest number of people—more than 4 billion. Asia also has the greatest percentage of the world's people—about 60 percent. That means that six out of ten people on Earth live in Asia. About 20 percent of the world's people live in one Asian country—China. Today, China has more people than any other country in the world.

Changes in Population Growth

After Africa, Asia has the world's second-fastest-growing population. In much of Asia, better health care is a reason for this growth. Men and women are living longer. There are fewer infant deaths. By 2025 India is expected to lead the world in population size. Great increases in population are expected in other South Asian countries, too. Many Arab countries in West Asia are also expected to have great population growth.

Some countries in East Asia are working to slow this growth. Because of land and food shortages, China's government has worked to slow its population growth. Today, China's couples are told to have only one child. Couples in Japan and South Korea are having fewer children by choice. The populations of China, Japan, and South Korea are predicted to decrease by 2050.

Asia's elderly are living longer. This contributes to the continent's large population.

Where Asia's People Live

Most of Asia's people live in river valleys and along coastlines. Asia's major cities were built as ports along the coasts. Asia's coastlines and deltas also provide good land for farming. Asia's rivers are sources of life to its people. The people depend on the rivers for drinking water, for irrigation water for crops, and as trade and transportation routes. The rich soil in the river valleys helps farmers grow great amounts of food crops.

About 55 percent of Asia's people live in rural areas. In some countries, that number is much higher. For example, more than 70 percent of the people in Afghanistan, India, and Thailand live in rural areas—mostly in farming villages and small towns. A few of them live in tents. They move from place to place as they graze their livestock on fresh patches of grass.

The other 45 percent of Asia's people live in or near large cities. Of course, some countries have a greater percentage of urban dwellers. Iran, Japan, South Korea, and most countries on the Arabian Peninsula are more than 80 percent urban. By 2030 about 55 percent of Asians will be living in cities. More Asians are completing high school and college. The jobs they want are found in the cities.

Some Asians are seeking jobs in cities in other Asian countries. For example, people from Pakistan and India are working in Saudi Arabia and in the United Arab Emirates.

Endangered Cultures

Besides endangered plants and animals, people from some of Asia's small ethnic groups are also endangered. Although the people themselves are not becoming extinct, their languages and cultures are. These people live in Asia's least-populated areas. When people from a larger ethnic group move in and develop an area, the members of the smaller ethnic group adopt the language and culture of the larger group.

About fifteen languages spoken only in Siberia are almost extinct. When logging companies cut down Siberia's forests, the forests' people lost their traditional homelands and way of life. Many of those people moved into towns. There, they started speaking the language and adopting the culture of the towns' people.

Expanding Cities

Besides gaining more people, Asia's cities continue to expand to cover more land. In China, India, Japan, and South Korea, cities now are nearer to rural areas. Rural people can remain in their home villages and still work in the now-nearby cities.

About 45 percent of all of Asia's people live in or near its cities.

China, South Korea, and Indonesia are trying something new. They are moving companies, jobs, and people from large cities to smaller ones. This lessens some of the demands put on the large cities to provide electricity, sewage processing, and other services for the people.

Asia's cities have also grown by actually increasing their land area. Singapore is both a city and one of Asia's smallest countries. It continues to add land to its shores by dredging sand from the sea. Other coastal Asian cities have done this, too. With rising sea levels, however, some of those newly created areas will likely sink or flood.

Palm Islands in the Persian Gulf

Located on the Persian Gulf, Dubai is part of the United Arab Emirates in West Asia. To increase tourism, Dubai's leaders decided to build three islands in the shape of palm trees. Altogether, the islands added 323 miles (520 km) of beaches to Dubai's coast.

The best-known island is Palm Jumeirah. About 40,000 workers from South Asia built it. They dug about 3.3 billion cubic feet (94 million cubic meters) of sand from the Persian Gulf. They also used about 7 million tons (6.3 t) of rock. This is the world's largest artificial island.

The island has had ups and downs. On the plus side, more sea plants and animals have moved into the water around the island. On the minus side, reports show that the island is sinking about 0.2 inches (0.5 cm) a year.

SIX
LOOKING FOR SOLUTIONS TO PRESENT-DAY PROBLEMS

Asia's growing population has a limited amount of usable, livable land. Overuse of that land has damaged some of the natural environment and caused changes in Asia's climate. Some of Asia's leaders and people are now working to correct those problems.

Asia's Major Problems

One of Asia's main problems is its large and still-growing population. Even though many families in East Asia are having fewer children, experts predict that the population throughout Asia as a whole will continue to increase. The people must go somewhere. Many will continue to move to urban areas in search of work. This will further overload the existing cities. City leaders will have to find more sources of clean water and ways to provide electricity for the growing populations. New cities will continue to be built. Some will develop in the deserts and steppes, where water is already scarce.

Another problem is education. In many Asian countries, education is not reaching everyone. Most Asian countries require children ages seven through fourteen to attend school. Many countries, however, have few schools and teachers. In some countries, girls are not allowed to go to school. In countries where women finish high school and college, they marry later and have fewer children. Therefore, increasing education for women could help slow Asia's population growth.

Unlike these boys, many children in Asia do not attend school.

Kothapally Village in India

Every year, the people in Kothapally Village in southeastern India ran out of water during the dry season. Every day, the village's women walked several miles to find water for drinking and cooking. Crops dried out in the fields. The land became hard and dry. When the monsoon rains came, the hard ground could not absorb the water fast enough. Much of the valuable rainwater that fell was wasted.

In 1999 the villagers began to work with a group of scientists. They learned how to build ponds and wells for collecting and storing the rainwater. They laid pipes that brought the water to the fields during the dry season. Today, crops grow year-round in Kothapally. The farmers plant more kinds of crops—cotton, rice, spices, and vegetables. They now also raise cows and sell milk.

The people of Kothapally have improved their lives and their environment. Their incomes have increased, too. The village women no longer spend most of their time looking for water and therefore can do other types of work. In addition, Kothapally's success has been televised throughout India. Farmers in other villages are now building their own ponds and wells.

Sanitation is another problem. Many people do not have modern plumbing with indoor toilets and running water. This makes it hard for them to wash themselves, their food, and their clothes. In many Asian countries, human waste is deposited in streams or left on the ground. Those unhealthy practices add to the spread of diseases.

Climate change is yet another problem that Asians must face. Throughout the twenty-first century, scientists expect Asia's climate to change even more. Asia will continue to grow warmer at a faster rate than the rest of world. East Asia will have longer and more frequent summer heat waves. South Asia will have fewer very cold days. Summer rains will decrease in already dry West and Central Asia. Rainfall will increase throughout the rest of Asia, causing severe floods. Cyclones and typhoons will bring even more rain and stronger winds to East, South, and Southeast Asia.

Toward a Better Tomorrow

Asia does have several things in its favor. Even Asia's large population can be an advantage. Asia has a large, eager workforce. Its people could be put to work replanting forests or building sewage-treatment systems. Asia's large population has also produced a number of well-educated people. Some of them were educated in Asia's universities. Others received degrees from schools in Australia, Europe, and North America. Asia's well-educated leaders and strong workforce are needed to help solve the continent's many problems.

Asia also has a great percentage of the world's natural resources within its vast landmass. North, Central, and West Asia have the world's largest oil deposits. North Asia has huge deposits of natural gas. Large deposits of coal, iron ore, gold, copper, and other metals needed in manufacturing are located throughout Asia. Southeast Asia has huge tin deposits and most of the world's rubber trees. Despite overcutting, North and Southeast Asia still have vast stretches of untouched forests.

In an effort to protect the environment, tree planting programs take place across the continent of Asia.

With well-educated leaders, a large workforce, and plentiful natural resources, Asia should be able to adopt programs to improve the environment. Already there have been successful attempts to stop desertification. Syria, India, and China have tree-planting programs in place to hold back the deserts. China even pays some farmers to plant trees rather than crops. Many countries with large forests have created nature reserves and national parks. In those areas, trees, other plant life, animals, and bodies of water are protected. The addition of trees and other plants should improve the air quality and lessen the results of climate change in Asia.

GLOSSARY

climate change   an increase or decrease in temperature or rainfall over a long period of time

continent   a large land mass

cyclone   a storm with damaging winds and heavy rain that hits lands bordering the Indian Ocean

deforestation   cutting down of entire forests

delta   the mouth of a river

desertification   weakening of the soil from deforestation, drought, overuse of land, or climate change

drought   a long period of time with little or no rainfall, making it hard to grow crops

endangered species   a plant or animal that is in danger of becoming extinct

erosion   the wearing away of land or soil by the action of water and wind

gorge — a deep river valley with steep, rocky sides

habitat — the natural place in which a plant or animal lives

monsoon — a strong wind that brings hot, wet weather to Asia in the summer and dry, cold weather in the winter

open-pit mine — a huge hole dug by miners and from which minerals are removed

permafrost — land that is permanently frozen beneath the ground's surface

reservoir — the body of water, usually a lake, that forms behind a dam

tectonic plates — the hard sheets of moving rock that make up Earth's crust

tsunami — a huge, damaging wave caused by an underwater earthquake

typhoon — a storm with damaging winds and heavy rain that hits lands bordering Asia's Pacific coast

FIND OUT MORE

BOOKS

Aloian, Molly. *The Himalayas*. New York: Crabtree Publishing Company, 2011.

Latham, Donna. *Tundra*. White River, Vermont: Nomad Press, 2010.

Leavitt, Amie. *Threat to the Yangtze River Dolphin*. Hockessin, Delaware: Mitchell Lane Publishers, 2008.

Woodward, John. *Climate Change*. New York: DK Publishing, 2008.

DVDS

Wild Asia: At the Edge, Life at the Vertical Limit. Razor Digital Entertainment, 2010.

Wild Asia: The Arid Heart. Razor Digital Entertainment, 2010.

WEBSITES

Asia Trail for Kids
http://nationalzoo.si.edu/Animals/AsiaTrail/asiaforkids.cfm
This is part of the Smithsonian National Zoo website. Learn about the Asian animals that live at the zoo, and find information about other Asian animals, as well.

Asia Weather
http://weather.org/asia.htm
This page shows current weather conditions across Asia, with links to the weather in each Asian country.

INDEX

Patricia K. Kummer has a B.A. in history from St. Catherine University in St. Paul, Minnesota, and an M.A. in history from Marquette University in Milwaukee, Wisconsin. She has written chapters about Asia for several world history textbooks and has authored books about the Asian countries of Jordan, North Korea, Singapore, South Korea, Syria, Thailand, and Tibet. In addition, she has written books about other countries, states, natural wonders, and inventions. Books she has written for Cavendish Square Publishing include *Working Horses* in the Horses! series and all seven books in the Climates and Continents series.